EASY HOMEMADI TREATS COOKBOOK

Irresistible Healthy and Nutrient-Packed Recipes Your Furry Friend Will Love

Contents

Meat-Based Treats 6
Chicken and Liver Treats 7
Beef and Carrot Bites 8
Turkey and Sweet Potato Balls 9
Chicken and Kale Bars 10
Beef and Blueberry Drops 11
Turkey and Cranberry Snacks 12
Lamb and Spinach Squares 13
Ground Meat & Veggies Kebab 14
Turkey and Apple Rings 15
Beef and Green Bean Bars 16
Turkey and Cranberry Drops 17
Lamb and Apple Bars 18
Dehydrated ground beef dog treats 19
Crunchy beef bones 20
Chicken and Sweet Potato Balls 21
Goat heart jerky dog treats 22
Lamb Kidney Bites 23
Lamb and Pea Cookies 24
Cheesy Chicken Dog Treats 25
Oatmeal Turkey Dog Treats 26
Fish-Based Treats 27
Chicken and Broccoli Bites 28
Dried Shrimp 29
Crab Cakes 30
Salmon Sushi 31
Salmon and Blueberry Drops 32
Boneless Sardine Sushi 33
Smoked Salmon with Cream Cheese 34
Tuna and Carrot Bites 35
Tuna and Cranberry Snacks 36
Sardine and Broccoli Bites 37
Salmon and Pea Bars 38
Fish Stew for Dogs 39
Vegetable-Based Treats 40
Carrot and Parsley Biscuits 41
Coconut Chips dog treats 42
Spinach and Sweet Potato Squares 43
Pea and Carrot Balls 44
Sweet Potato and Cranberry Bites 45
Lentil and Spinach Bars 46
Chickpea and Pumpkin Cookies 47
Banana Oatmeal Dog Treats 48
Broccoli and Apple Squares 49
Spinach and Blueberry Biscuits 50
Special Diet Treats 51
Allergy-Friendly Chicken and Rice Cookies 52
Very Berry Low Fat Dog Treats 53
Grilled Sweet Potato 54
Digestive-Friendly Pumpkin and Ginger Treats 55
Turkey and Green Bean Bites 56
Low-Fat Chicken and Carrot Bars 57
Dental Health Beef and Parsley Jerky 58
Low-Calorie Tuna and Cucumber Bites 59
Joint Health Lamb and Turmeric Cookies 60
Skin and Coat Chicken and Coconut Bars 61
Grain-Sensitive Sweet Potato and Quinoa Biscuits. 62
Diabetic-Friendly Chicken and Apple Treats 63
Gluten-Free Beef and Potato Squares 64
Vegetarian Lentil and Carrot Balls 65
Picky Eater Chicken and Cheese Bars 66
Snacks Treats 67
Peanut Butter and Banana Biscuits 68
Cheesy Bacon Bites 69
Chicken and Rice Balls 70
Carrot and Apple Cookies 71
Sweet Potato and Cinnamon Treats 72
Blueberry and Yogurt Squares 73
Beef and Cheddar Bars 74
Fried Fish Skin 75
Air Fried Pork Rinds 76
Salmon and Dill Biscuits 77
Dried Beef Stomach 78
Air Fried Bacon Strips 79
Carrot and Cheese Treats 80
Dry Dog Snack 81
Peanut Butter Carob Cups 82
Grain Free Treats 83
Bully Sticks 84
Sweet Potato and Turkey Jerky 85
Chickpea and Carrot Balls 86
Dried Beef Lungs 87
Dog Cupcakes 88
Fried Beef Liver 89
Chickpea and Blueberry Squares 90
Lentil and Broccoli Cookies 91
Peanut Butter and Pumpkin Bones 92
Chickpea and Beef Brownies 93

Introduction

Dear Fellow Dog Lover,

Have you ever been in the pet food aisle of the store, overwhelmed by the endless selection of dog treats, only to be disappointed by the questionable ingredients and the lack of transparency in the pet food industry? Are you tired of wondering whether the treats you give your dog are truly good or if they do more harm than good? You've come to the right place if you're as concerned about your beloved canine companion's health and well-being as I am.

As a passionate dog owner and a dedicated advocate for natural, healthy nutrition, I've been on a quest to revolutionize how we feed our pets. The journey began when Penny, my precious Labrador, developed mysterious health problems that seemed exacerbated by the usual dog food and treats. I've been fed up with the animal feed business and its need for more transparency. At that moment, I decided to take matters into my own hands and make Penny's dog treats on my own.

But why would you make these dog treats at home instead of buying them in a store? First, you have complete control over the ingredients, which means you know precisely what your dog is eating. This book provides recipes using wholesome, natural ingredients. No more mystery meats, artificial colors, or harmful preservatives - just real food for your best friend. Plus, your dog's unique dietary needs and preferences can be considered when creating his treats so he gets the best nutrition possible.

Penny's condition improved, and my homemade dog treats brought us closer together. It was a labor of love for me to create and share these recipes to show Penny how much she meant to me. Now I'd like to share that love with you and your dog.

Are you ready to leave the pet food industry behind and embark on a journey to strengthen your bond with your furry friend and give him the nutritious, natural treats he deserves? If your answer is yes, then let's take this journey together. With this book, you can create delicious, healthy snacks that will keep your dog's tail wagging for more!
I wish you and your beloved canine companion a lifetime of health, happiness, and wagging tails,

Emma

Meat-Based Treats

Chicken and Liver Treats

40 minutes

12-16 Treats

NUTRITIONAL VALUES

Calories: 60, Protein: 6g, Fat: 2g, Carbohydrates: 4g, Fiber: 1g, Sugar: 1g

INGREDIENTS

1 lb boneless, skinless chicken breasts
1/2 cup chicken liver
1 cup rolled oats
1/2 cup grated carrot
1/4 cup chopped parsley
1 egg

DIRECTIONS

1. Prepare a parchment-lined baking sheet and preheat the oven to 350°F (175°C).
2. Combine chicken liver and chicken breast chunks in a food processor. Pulse to powder.
3. Mix the ground chicken, liver, rolled oats, shredded carrot, chopped parsley, and egg in a large bowl. Stir well for a thick, wet dough.
4. Place dough balls on the baking sheet using a tablespoon or tiny biscuit scoop.
5. Bake for 25 to 30 mins, or until the top is golden brown and the inside is done.
6. Before feeding your dog, let the goodies cool.
7. Freeze or refrigerate the snacks for up to 3 months.

Beef and Carrot Bites

40 minutes

12-16 Treats

NUTRITIONAL VALUES

Calories: 70, Protein: 7g, Fat: 3g, Carbohydrates: 3g, Fiber: 1g, Sugar: 1g

INGREDIENTS

1 lb ground beef
1/2 cup grated carrot
1/4 cup chopped parsley
1 egg
1/2 cup rolled oats

DIRECTIONS

1. Prepare a parchment-lined baking sheet and preheat the oven to 350°F (175°C).
2. Mix ground beef, shredded carrot, chopped parsley, egg and rolled oats. Stir well for a thick, wet dough.
3. Place dough balls on the baking sheet using a tablespoon or tiny biscuit scoop.
4. Bake for 20 to 25 mins, until golden brown and well done.
5. Before feeding your dog, let the goodies cool.
6. Freeze or refrigerate the snacks for up to 3 months.

Turkey and Sweet Potato Balls

35 minutes

12-16 Treats

NUTRITIONAL VALUES

Calories: 60, Protein: 6g, Fat: 2g, Carbohydrates: 4g, Fiber: 1g, Sugar: 1g

INGREDIENTS

1 lb ground turkey
1/2 cup mashed sweet potato
1/4 cup chopped parsley
1 egg
1/2 cup almond flour
1 tsp ground cinnamon (optional)

DIRECTIONS

1. Prepare a parchment-lined baking sheet and preheat the oven to 350°F (175°C).
2. Mix ground turkey, sweet potato, parsley, egg, almond flour, and cinnamon in a large basin (if using). Stir well for a thick, wet dough.
3. Place dough balls on the baking sheet using a tablespoon or tiny biscuit scoop.
4. Put in the oven and cook for 20-25 minutes or until golden brown and fully done.
5. Before feeding your dog, let the goodies cool.
6. Freeze or refrigerate the snacks for up to 3 months.

Chicken and Kale Bars

40 minutes

12-16 Treats

NUTRITIONAL VALUES

Calories: 60, Protein: 6g, Fat: 2g, Carbohydrates: 5g, Fiber: 2g, Sugar: 1g

INGREDIENTS

1 lb boneless, skinless chicken breasts
1/2 cup chopped kale
1/4 cup chopped cilantro
1 egg
1/2 cup coconut flour
1 tsp turmeric powder (optional)

DIRECTIONS

1. Set the oven temperature to 350°F (175°C). Line a baking tray with parchment.
2. Chop the chicken breasts into small pieces and combine them with the greens and cilantro in a food processor. Pulse until pulverized.
3. Combine the ground chicken and kale mixture with the egg, coconut flour, and turmeric powder in a large mixing bowl (if using). Stir thoroughly to make a dense, moist dough.
4. Evenly press the dough into a baking dish and smooth the surface.
5. Bake for 20-25 mins or until golden brown and cooked through.
6. Let the bars fully cool before slicing them into little squares.
7. Refrigerate the treats in an airtight container for up to one week, or freeze them for up to three months.

Beef and Blueberry Drops

35 minutes

12 treats

NUTRITIONAL VALUES

Calories: 70, Protein: 7g, Fat: 3g, Carbohydrates: 4g, Fiber: 1g, Sugar: 1g

INGREDIENTS

1 lb ground beef
1/2 cup blueberries, mashed
1/4 cup chopped parsley
1 egg
1/2 cup almond flour
1 tsp dried rosemary (optional)

DIRECTIONS

1. Set the oven to 350°F (175°C), and use parchment paper to cover a baking sheet.
2. Mix ground beef, mashed blueberries, minced parsley, egg, almond flour, and dry rosemary in a bowl (if using). Stir well for a thick, wet dough.
3. A tablespoon or small biscuit scoop drops the dough on the baking sheet.
4. Bake for 20 to 25 mins, until golden brown and well done.
5. Before feeding your dog, let the goodies cool.
6. Freeze or refrigerate the snacks for up to 3 months.

Turkey and Cranberry Snacks

40 minutes | **12-16 Treats**

NUTRITIONAL VALUES

Calories: 70, Protein: 7g, Fat: 2g, Carbohydrates: 5g, Fiber: 2g, Sugar: 2g

INGREDIENTS

1 lb ground turkey
1/2 cup dried cranberries, chopped
1/4 cup chopped sage
1 egg
1/2 cup coconut flour
1 tsp ground ginger (optional

DIRECTIONS

1. Set the oven temperature to 350°F (175°C). Line a baking tray with parchment.
2. Mix ground turkey, chopped dried cranberries, chopped sage, egg, coconut flour, and ground ginger (if using). Make a thick, moist dough by mixing.
3. Use a tablespoon or tiny biscuit scoop to form dough balls on the baking sheet.
4. Use a fork to press the balls down into a little flatter shape.
5. Bake for 15-20 minutes until it gets golden brown and done.

Lamb and Spinach Squares

50 minutes

12-16 Treats

NUTRITIONAL VALUES

Calories: 80, Protein: 8g, Fat: 4g, Carbohydrates: 4g, Fiber: 1g, Sugar: 1g

INGREDIENTS

1 lb ground lamb
1/2 cup chopped spinach
1/4 cup chopped mint
1 egg
1/2 cup oat flour
1 tsp ground coriander (optional)

DIRECTIONS

1. Set the oven temperature to 350°F (175°C) and line a baking dish with a cookie sheet.
2. Mix ground lamb, spinach, mint, egg, oat flour, and coriander in a large basin (if using). Stir well for a thick, wet dough.
3. Evenly press the dough into the prepared baking dish and smooth the surface.
4. Bake for 30-35 minutes or till golden brown and cooked through.
5. Let the squares cool to room temperature before slicing them into little pieces.
6. Freeze or refrigerate the snacks for up to 3 months.

Ground Meat & Veggies Kebab

30 minutes

4-6 kebabs

NUTRITIONAL VALUES

Calories: 170, Protein: 23g, Fat: 4g, Carbohydrates: 9g, Fiber: 2g

INGREDIENTS

1 lb. ground beef, chicken, or turkey
1 cup mixed vegetables (bell peppers, zucchini, cherry tomatoes)
8-12 wooden or metal skewers

DIRECTIONS

1. Preheat your grill to medium heat.
2. Form the ground meat into small meatballs and thread them onto the skewers, alternating with the mixed vegetables.
3. Grill and cook for 13-15 minutes, turning occasionally, until the meat is cooked thoroughly.
4. Allow the ground meat & veggies kebabs to cool before serving.

Turkey and Apple Rings

45 minutes

12-16 Treats

NUTRITIONAL VALUES

Calories: 70, Protein: 7g, Fat: 2g, Carbohydrates: 5g, Fiber: 1g, Sugar: 2g

INGREDIENTS

1 lb ground turkey
1/2 cup grated apple
1/4 cup chopped thyme
1 egg
1/2 cup oat flour
1 tsp ground nutmeg (optional)

DIRECTIONS

1. Turn the oven to 350°F (175°C) and put parchment paper on a baking sheet.
2. Mix ground turkey, grated apple, chopped thyme, egg, oat flour, and ground nutmeg in a large basin (if using). Stir well for a thick, wet dough.
3. Form dough rings and set them on the baking sheet.
4. Bake for 25 to 30 mins, or until the top is golden brown and the inside is done.
5. Before feeding your dog, let the goodies cool.
6. Freeze or refrigerate the snacks for up to 3 months.

Beef and Green Bean Bars

55 minutes | **12-16 Treats**

NUTRITIONAL VALUES

Calories: 70, Protein: 8g, Fat: 3g, Carbohydrates: 4g, Fiber: 1g, Sugar: 1g

INGREDIENTS

1 lb ground beef
1/2 cup chopped green beans
1/4 cup chopped rosemary
1 egg
1/2 cup almond flour
1 tsp smoked paprika (optional)

DIRECTIONS

1. Set the oven temperature to 350°F (175°C) and prepare a baking dish with waxed paper.
2. Mix ground beef, chopped green beans, chopped rosemary, egg, almond flour, and smoked paprika in a large bowl (if using). For a dense, moist dough, stir well.
3. Smooth the dough into the baking dish that has been prepared.
4. Bake for 37-40 minutes until golden brown and cooked through.
5. Cut the bars into small pieces after letting them cool to room temperature.
6. Keep the goodies in an airtight jar in the fridge for 1 week or freeze them for 3 months.

Turkey Coconut Ball Dog Treats

35 minutes | **30 Treats**

NUTRITIONAL VALUES

Calories: 35, Protein: 3g, Fat: 2g, Carbohydrates: 1g, Fiber: 0.5g, Sugar: 0.5g

INGREDIENTS

1 pound ground turkey
1 cup cooked brown rice
½ cup canned pumpkin puree
¼ cup unsweetened shredded coconut
1 egg
1 tsp dried parsley
¼ cup unsweetened shredded coconut (for rolling)t

DIRECTIONS

1. Preheat your oven to 350°F (175°C). Combine the ground turkey with cooked brown rice, canned pumpkin puree, ¼ cup of shredded coconut, egg, and dried parsley in a bowl. Mix well until all are fully incorporated.
2. Roll the mixture into small, bite-sized balls about the size of a marble. Place the turkey balls onto a baking sheet lined with parchment paper. Bake in the preheated oven for 17-20 minutes or until the turkey is cooked.
3. Let the turkey balls cool for a few minutes, then roll them in the remaining ¼ cup of shredded coconut until fully coated. Let the treats cool completely before serving them to your furry friend.

Lamb and Apple Bars

55 minutes

12-16 Treats

NUTRITIONAL VALUES

Calories: 70, Protein: 7g, Fat: 3g, Carbohydrates: 4g, Fiber: 2g, Sugar: 1g

INGREDIENTS

1 lb ground lamb
1/2 cup grated apple
1/4 cup chopped mint
1 egg
1/2 cup coconut flour
1 tsp ground ginger (optional)

DIRECTIONS

1. Prepare a wax paper baking dish and preheat the oven to 350°F (175°C).
2. Mix ground lamb, grated apple, chopped mint, egg, coconut flour, and ground ginger in a large bowl (if using). Stir well for a thick, wet dough.
3. Evenly press the dough into the prepared baking dish and smooth the surface.
4. Bake for 35 to 40 minutes, until golden brown and thoroughly done.
5. After cooling, cut the bars into small pieces.
6. Freeze or refrigerate the snacks for up to 3 months.

Dehydrated ground beef dog treats

10 hours | **20-25 Treats**

NUTRITIONAL VALUES

Calories: 45, Protein: 3.6g, Fat: 3.2g, Carbohydrates: 0.7g Cholesterol: 22mg

INGREDIENTS

1 pound ground beef
1 tablespoon coconut oil
1/2 cup grated carrots
1/4 cup chopped parsley
1 egg

DIRECTIONS

1. Set your oven to 350°F (180°C) and turn it on. Mix the ground beef, coconut oil, grated carrot, chopped parsley, and egg in a large bowl.
2. Mix well until all of the ingredients are well blended.
3. Spread the mixture out evenly on parchment paper on a baking sheet.
4. Put the baking tray in the oven and bake for 10 to 15 minutes or until the beef is fully cooked.
5. Remove the beef from the oven and allow it to cool.
6. Once cooled, grind the beef into small pieces using a food processor or blender.
7. Preheat your dehydrator to 160°F (71°C).
8. Spread the ground beef onto dehydrator trays in a thin, even layer.
9. Place the trays into the dehydrator and let them dry for 8-10 hours or until the beef is completely dry and crispy.
10. Once the beef is fully dehydrated, please remove it from the trays and store it in an airtight container.

Crunchy beef bones

3 hours | **10-12 Treats**

NUTRITIONAL VALUES

Fat:4g, Carbohydrates: 14g, Fiber: 2g, Sugar: 0.5g, Protein: 5g

INGREDIENTS

1 cup whole wheat flour
1/2 cup beef broth
1/2 cup rolled oats
1/4 cup cornmeal
1/4 cup ground flaxseed
1 egg
1/4 cup chopped parsley
1/4 cup grated parmesan cheese

DIRECTIONS

1. Preheat the oven to 350°F (180°C). Add the whole wheat flour, beef broth, rolled oats, cornmeal, ground flaxseed, egg, chopped parsley, and grated parmesan cheese in a large mixing basin.
2. Stir items together until thoroughly mixed. On a roughly floured surface, roll out the dough to a 1/4-inch thickness.
3. Cut the goodies into the desired form and size, such as bone shapes, using a cookie cutter.
4. Place the treats on a baking sheet lined with parchment paper. Bake in the preheated oven for 2-3 hours or until the treats are hard and crunchy.
5. Remove the treats from the oven and allow them to cool completely before serving.

Chicken and Sweet Potato Balls

40 minutes

12-16 Treats

NUTRITIONAL VALUES

Calories: 60, Protein: 6g, Fat: 2g, Carbohydrates: 4g, Fiber: 2g, Sugar: 1g

INGREDIENTS

1 lb boneless, skinless chicken breasts
1/2 cup mashed sweet potato
1/4 cup chopped parsley
1 egg
1/2 cup almond flour
1 tsp ground paprika (optional)

DIRECTIONS

1. Prepare a parchment-lined baking sheet and preheat the oven to 350°F (175°C).
2. Put the mashed sweet potato, minced parsley, and chicken breast bits in a food processor. Pulse to powder.
3. Mix the ground chicken, sweet potato, egg, almond flour, and ground paprika in a large basin (if using). Stir well for a thick, wet dough.
4. Place dough balls on the baking sheet using a tablespoon or tiny biscuit scoop.
5. Bake for 23-25 minutes, until golden brown and well done.
6. Let the treats cool completely before giving them to your dog.
7. Freeze or refrigerate the snacks for up to 3 months.

Goat heart jerky dog treats

6 hours

10-12 Treats

NUTRITIONAL VALUES

Calories: 84, Fat: 2.4g, Carbohydrates: 2.2g, Fiber: 0g, Sugar: 2.1g, Protein: 13.4g

INGREDIENTS

1 pound goat heart, sliced into thin strips
1/4 cup apple cider vinegar
2 tbsp honey
1 tsp smoked paprika

DIRECTIONS

1. Whisk the apple cider vinegar, honey and smoked paprika in a large bowl.
2. Slice the goat heart and add it to the bowl. Toss the meat to coat it evenly.
3. Put the meat in the bowl, Put it in a plastic bag, and freeze it for at least two hours and up to a day.
4. Turn your oven on and set it to 175°F (80°C). Line a baking tray and arrange the marinated goat heart strips in a single layer.
5. Bake the jerky in an oven that has already been heated for 4 to 6 hours or until it is dry and crispy.
6. Once the jerky is cooked, please remove it from the oven and let it cool down completely before serving.
7. The jerky can be kept in the fridge for up to two weeks in a container that keeps air out.

Lamb Kidney Bites

3 hours

30-40 Treats

NUTRITIONAL VALUES

Calories: 22, Fat: 0.8g, Carbohydrates: 1.4g, Fiber: 0g, Sugar: 1.4g, Protein: 2.2g

INGREDIENTS

1 pound lamb kidneys
1/4 cup plain Greek yogurt
1 tbsp apple cider vinegar
1 tbsp honey
1/2 tsp dried oregano

DIRECTIONS

1. Bring the oven to a temperature of 200°F (90°C).
2. Lamb kidneys should be thoroughly soaked in water and patted dry with paper towels.
3. Shred the kidneys into manageable chunks.
4. Greek yogurt, ACV, honey, and dried oregano should be combined in a large mixing basin and whisked until smooth.
5. Toss in the pieces of lamb kidney to ensure an equal coating.
6. Line a baking sheet with parchment paper, and then spread out the kidney pieces in a single layer.
7. Bake the bits for at least two hours in a preheated oven to ensure the bits get dry and crispy.
8. After baking the bites, take them out and set them on a cooling rack to cool completely before serving.
9. Keep the bits in the fridge for up to a week in an airtight container.

Lamb and Pea Cookies

45 minutes

12-16 Treats

NUTRITIONAL VALUES

Calories: 70, Protein: 7g, Fat: 3g, Carbohydrates: 4g, Fiber: 1g, Sugar: 1g

INGREDIENTS

1 lb ground lamb
1/2 cup cooked peas
1/4 cup chopped mint
1 egg
1/2 cup oat flour
1 tsp ground cumin (optional)

DIRECTIONS

1. Heat the oven to 350°F (175°C) and put parchment paper on a baking sheet.
2. Mix ground lamb, cooked peas, mint, egg, oat flour, and ground cumin in a large bowl (if using). Stir well for a thick, wet dough.
3. Place dough balls on the baking sheet using a tablespoon or tiny biscuit scoop.
4. Bake for 27-30 minutes until it gets golden brown and done.
5. Please wait until the treats are completely cool before giving them to your dog.
6. Freeze or refrigerate the snacks for up to 3 months.

Cheesy Chicken Dog Treats

45 minutes

30-40 Treats

NUTRITIONAL VALUES

Calories: 84, Fat: 2.4g, Carbohydrates: 2.2g, Fiber: 0g, Sugar: 2.1g, Protein: 13.4g

INGREDIENTS

1 cup cooked, shredded chicken
1/2 cup oat flour
1/2 cup shredded cheddar cheese
1 egg
2 tbsp chopped fresh parsley
2 tbsp water

DIRECTIONS

1. Set the temperature of your oven to 350°F (180°C).
2. Shred the cooked chicken and add it to a large mixing bowl along with the oat flour, cheddar cheese, egg, minced parsley, and water.
3. Combine all of the ingredients by mixing them thoroughly.
4. Roll out the dough until gets thick of about 1/4 inch on a roughly floured surface.
5. Make snacks in the form of bones or any other shape you like using a cookie cutter of the appropriate size.
6. Put the goodies on a parchment paper-lined baking sheet.
7. Bake in the oven preheated oven for 27-30 minutes or until the treats are golden brown.
8. Take the goodies out of the oven and let them cool to room temperature before serving.
9. The snacks can last for a week if stored in the refrigirator in an airtight container.

Oatmeal Turkey Dog Treats

45 minutes

30-40 Treats

NUTRITIONAL VALUES

Calories: 63, Fat: 1.6g, Carbohydrates: 9.7g, Fiber: 1.3g, Sugar: 1.8g, Protein: 3.5g

INGREDIENTS

1 cup cooked, shredded turkey
1 1/2 cups oat flour
1/2 cup rolled oats
1/4 cup unsweetened applesauce
1/4 cup water
1 egg
1 tbsp honey

DIRECTIONS

1. Preheat the oven to 350°F (180°C).
2. Mix the cooked, shredded turkey, oat flour, rolled oats, unsweetened applesauce, water, egg, and honey in a large mixing bowl.
3. Stir items together until thoroughly mixed.
4. Roll out the dough to a 1/4-inch thickness on a floured surface.
5. Cut the goodies into the desired form and size, such as bone shapes, using a cookie cutter.
6. Place the treats on a baking tray lined with parchment paper.
7. Bake the goodies in a preheated oven for 27-30 mintues or until golden brown.
8. Before serving, remove the treats from the oven and allow them to cool fully.
9. Refrigerate the treats in an airtight container for up to one week.

Fish-Based Treats

Salmon Shabu Fish Dog Treat

40 minutes

20 Treats

NUTRITIONAL VALUES

Calories: 45, Protein: 3g, Fat: 2g, Carbohydrates: 3g, Fiber: 1g, Sugar: 0.5g

INGREDIENTS

1 pound salmon fillets, skin removed
1 can (15 oz weight) chickpeas, drained and rinsed
¼ cup chopped sweet potatoes
2 eggs
¼ cup coconut flour
¼ cup ground flaxseed
¼ teaspoon turmeric powder
¼ teaspoon dried rosemary

DIRECTIONS

1. Preheat your oven to 350°F (175°C). In a food blender, pulse the salmon fillets until coarsely ground. Add chickpeas and chopped sweet potatoes to the food blender. Pulse until the chickpeas and sweet potatoes are finely chopped and well combined with the salmon.
2. Transfer the salmon and chickpea mixture to the bowl. Add eggs with coconut flour, ground flaxseed, turmeric powder, and dried rosemary to the mixing bowl. Mix well until all are fully incorporated.
3. Use a fish-shaped cookie cutter to cut or shape the batter into a fish. Place the fish-shaped treats onto the paper-arranged baking sheet. Bake for 23-25 minutes until the treats are firm and lightly browned. Let the treats cool completely before serving them to your furry friend.

Dried Shrimp

8-10 hours

5 oz

NUTRITIONAL VALUES

Calories: 350, Protein: 25g, Fat: 9g, Carbohydrates: 45g, Fiber: 6g

INGREDIENTS

1 lb. fresh or thawed shrimp, peeled and deveined

DIRECTIONS

1. Preheat your oven to 170°F (77°C) or the lowest possible setting.
2. Arrange the shrimp on a wire rack placed on a baking sheet.
3. Bake for 8-10 hours or until the shrimp are fully dried and crisp.
4. Allow the dried shrimp to cool before serving.

Crab Cakes

25 minutes

7-8 Treats

NUTRITIONAL VALUES

Calories: 60, Protein: 5g, Fat: 3g, Carbohydrates: 5g, Fiber: 1g, Sugar: 1g

INGREDIENTS

1 can of lump crab meat, drained
1 egg
1/2 cup of cooked sweet potato, mashed
1/4 cup of almond flour
1 tablespoon of chopped fresh parsley
1/4 teaspoon of ground turmeric

DIRECTIONS

1. Preheat your oven to 350°F (175°C).
2. In a large mixing bowl, combine the drained lump crab meat, egg, cooked and mashed sweet potato, almond flour, chopped fresh parsley, and ground turmeric.
3. Mix all the ingredients together until well combined.
4. Form the mixture into small, flattened cakes.
5. Place the crab cakes on a baking sheet lined with parchment paper.
6. Bake for 15-20 minutes, or until the crab cakes are golden brown and cooked through.
7. Allow the crab cakes to cool before serving.

Salmon Sushi

10 minutes | **10 treats**

NUTRITIONAL VALUES

Calories: 35, Protein: 2g, Fat: 1g, Carbohydrates: 4g, Fiber: 0g

INGREDIENTS

1/2 cup cooked white rice
2-3 oz cooked salmon, shredded
1 tablespoon of low-fat cream cheese
1 teaspoon of chopped fresh dill
1 teaspoon of salmon eggs

DIRECTIONS

1. Mix the cooked white rice with the shredded salmon and chopped fresh dill.
2. Lay a piece of plastic wrap on a flat surface.
3. Spread the cream cheese over the plastic wrap.
4. Spoon the rice and salmon mixture on top of the cream cheese, leaving a small border at the top and bottom.
5. Roll the sushi into a tight roll using the plastic wrap.
6. Cut the sushi into small pieces and top each piece with a small amount of salmon eggs.

Salmon and Blueberry Drops

55 minutes

35-40 Treats

NUTRITIONAL VALUES

Calories: 40, Protein: 3g, Fat: 1g, Carbohydrates: 4g, Fiber: 1g, Sugar: 0g

INGREDIENTS

1 pound of fresh salmon, skin removed and cut into small cubes
1 cup of whole wheat flour
1/4 cup of ground flaxseed
1/4 cup of unsweetened applesauce
2 eggs
1/4 cup of water

DIRECTIONS

1. Preheat your oven to 350°F (175°C).
2. In a large mixing bowl, combine the whole wheat flour and ground flaxseed.
3. In the other bowl, whisk the unsweetened applesauce, eggs, and water.
4. Add the wet ingredients to the dry ingredients and mix until well combined.
5. Fold in the cubed salmon until it is evenly distributed throughout the dough.
6. Form the mixture into small, bite-sized nuggets.
7. Place the nuggets on a baking sheet lined with parchment paper.
8. Bake for 17-20 minutes, or until the nuggets are golden brown and cooked through.
9. Allow the nuggets to cool before serving.
10. You can serve these salmon nuggets as a treat or as a meal topper for your dog's regular food.

Sardine Oatcakes

35 minutes

12 treats

NUTRITIONAL VALUES

Calories for two treats: 50, Protein: 3g, Fat: 2.5g, Carbohydrates: 4g, Fiber: 0.5g

INGREDIENTS

240g sardines in oil, drained and mashed
¼ cup whole meal flour
1¼ cups oats
150ml chicken broth
1 egg

DIRECTIONS

1. Preheat your oven to 350°F (175°C). Combine the mashed sardines, whole meal flour, oats, chicken broth, and egg in a bowl. Mix well until all elements are combined and form a dough.
2. On the lightly greased smooth surface, roll out to a thickness of about ¼-inch.
3. Use a cookie cutter (any shape) to cut out the treats. Put the treats on the paper-arranged baking sheet.
4. Bake for 23-25 minutes or until the treats are firm and lightly browned.
5. Cool the treats before serving them to your furry friend.

Smoked Salmon with Cream Cheese

10 minutes

8 Treats

NUTRITIONAL VALUES

Calories: 120, Protein: 10g, Fat: 4g, Carbohydrates: 10g, Fiber: 2g, Sugar: 2g

INGREDIENTS

1 slice of whole-grain bread
1 tablespoon of low-fat cream cheese
4 oz. of smoked salmon, shredded
A few sprigs of fresh parsley

DIRECTIONS

1. Toast the bread and allow it to cool.
2. Spread the cream cheese over the bread.
3. Sprinkle the shredded smoked salmon over the cream cheese.
4. Garnish with fresh parsley.

Note: Make sure to remove any bones from the smoked salmon before giving it to your dog.

Vegetable and Tuna Patties

35 minutes

12 Treats

NUTRITIONAL VALUES

Calories: 50, Protein: 4g, Fat: 1.5g, Carbohydrates: 6g, Fiber: 1g

INGREDIENTS

1 can tuna in water, drained
1 cup mixed vegetables, cooked and mashed
1 egg
¼ cup of chopped parsley (optional)

DIRECTIONS

1. Preheat your oven to 350°F (175°C). In a bowl, combine the drained tuna with mashed vegetables, egg, and chopped parsley (if using). Mix well until fully incorporated. Divide the mixture into small patties and put them on the paper-arranged baking sheet.
2. Bake for 23-25 minutes until the patties are firm and lightly browned. Cool completely before serving your pet.

Tuna and Cranberry Snacks

35 minutes

12-16 treats

NUTRITIONAL VALUES

Calories: 60, Protein: 7g, Fat: 1g, Carbohydrates: 5g, Fiber: 1g, Sugar: 2g

INGREDIENTS

1 lb canned tuna, drained
1/2 cup dried cranberries, chopped
1/4 cup chopped mint
1 egg
1/2 cup coconut flour
1 tsp ground cumin (optional)

DIRECTIONS

1. Prepare a parchment-lined baking sheet and preheat the oven to 350°F (175°C).
2. Mix the canned tuna, dried cranberries, mint, egg, coconut flour, and ground cumin in a large basin (if using). Stir well for a thick, wet dough.
3. Place dough balls on the baking sheet using a tablespoon or tiny biscuit scoop.
4. Use a spoon or fork to flatten the balls softly.
5. Bake for 20–25 minutes until the top gets golden brown and the center is done.
6. Before feeding your dog, let the goodies cool.
7. Freeze or refrigerate the snacks for up to 3 months.

Sardine and Broccoli Patty Treat

32 minutes

12 Treats

NUTRITIONAL VALUES

Calories: 158, Fat: 8g, Carbohydrates: 11g, Fiber: 3g, Sugars: 3g, Protein: 13g

INGREDIENTS

1 can of sardines, drained and mashed
1 cup of steamed broccoli, finely chopped
1 cup of grated carrots
¼ cup of breadcrumbs
Salt and pepper to taste
Cooking spray

DIRECTIONS

1. In a bowl, combine the mashed sardines with steamed broccoli, grated carrots, breadcrumbs, egg, salt, and pepper. Mix well (with masher) until all are evenly combined. Form the mixture into 4 evenly sized patties.
2. Preheat your air fryer to 375°F. Lightly coat the patties with cooking spray on both sides. Put the patties into the air fryer basket, making sure they are not touching each other. Cook the patties in the air fryer for 6 minutes.
3. Carefully flip the patties and cook for an additional 6 minutes or until the patties are golden brown and crispy. Once done, remove the patties from the air fryer and serve hot.

Dried Salmon Dog Treat

6-8 hours

50 Sticks

NUTRITIONAL VALUES

Calories: 50, Fat: 2g, Carbohydrates: 0g, Fiber: 0g, Sugars: 0g, Protein: 9g

INGREDIENTS

2 lb. fresh salmon fillet
Non-stick cooking spray

DIRECTIONS

1. Preheat your oven to 200°F. Arrange the baking sheet with parchment paper and lightly coat the paper with non-stick cooking spray. Cut the salmon fillet into thin strips, about ¼-inch in thickness.
2. Place the salmon strips onto the prepared baking sheet, ensuring they are not touching each other. Bake the salmon strips for 6-8 hours or until they are fully dried and crisp.
3. Once done, remove the salmon strips from the oven and allow them to cool completely. Store the dried salmon strips in an air-sealed container or plastic bag.

Fish & Peanut Butter Dog Treats

50 minutes | **30 heart-shaped treats**

NUTRITIONAL VALUES

Calories: 60, Protein: 3g, Fat: 2g, Carbohydrates: 8g, Fiber: 1g, Sugar: 0.5g

INGREDIENTS

2 cups whole wheat flour
½ cup ground rolled oats
½ cup ground flaxseed
½ cup fish (salmon or tuna any), cooked and flaked
¼ cup creamy peanut butter
2 eggs
½ cup water

DIRECTIONS

1. Preheat your oven to 350°F (175°C). Combine the whole wheat flour with ground oats and flaxseed in a bowl.
2. Mix well. Add cooked and flaked fish with creamy peanut butter, eggs, and water to the bowl. Mix until all ingredients are fully incorporated.
3. Roll the mixture out onto a floured surface to a thickness of about ¼-inch. Use a heart-shaped cutter or cookie cutter to cut out the treats.
4. Place the heart-shaped treats onto the paper-arranged baking sheet. Bake for 27-30 minutes until firm and lightly browned.
5. Cool the treats completely before serving them to your furry friend.

Vegetable-Based Treats

Carrot and Parsley Biscuits

30 minutes | **10-12 Treats**

NUTRITIONAL VALUES

Calories: 55, Protein: 2g, Fat: 1g, Carbohydrates: 10g, Fiber: 1g

INGREDIENTS

1 cup whole wheat flour
1/2 cup grated carrots
1/4 cup chopped fresh parsley
1/4 cup water
1 egg

DIRECTIONS

1. Prepare a parchment-lined baking sheet and preheat the oven to 350°F (175°C).
2. Combine flour, grated carrots, and parsley in a medium bowl.
3. Whisk water and egg in a small bowl.
4. Mix wet and dry ingredients to make dough.
5. Cut biscuits from the 1/4-inch dough using a biscuit cutter.
6. Bake the biscuits for 20 minutes until golden.
7. Allow cooling completely before serving.

Coconut Chips Dog Treats

30 minutes

20 Treats

NUTRITIONAL VALUES

Calories: 47, Fat: 3.7g, Carbohydrates: 2.4g, Fiber: 1.4g, Sugar: 0.4g, Protein: 1.5g

INGREDIENTS

1 cup Coconut Chips
1/2 cup coconut flour
2 eggs
1/4 cup coconut oil
1/4 cup water
1/4 cup shredded carrot

DIRECTIONS

1. Set the oven temperature to 350°F (180°C). Combine the Coconut Chips and coconut flour in a large mixing bowl. Whisk together the eggs, coconut oil, shredded carrot and water in another dish.
2. Combine the wet and dry ingredients to form a dough.
3. Roll out the dough to a 1/4-inch thickness on a roughly floured surface.
4. Use a cookie cutter to cut the goodies into the desired shape and size.
5. Place the treats on a baking tray lined with parchment paper.
6. Bake the treats in the oven for 20 minutes or until golden brown.
7. Before serving, remove the treats from the oven and allow them to cool fully.

Spinach and Sweet Potato Squares

40 minutes

16-18 Treats

NUTRITIONAL VALUES

Calories: 55, Protein: 2g, Fat: 1g, Carbohydrates: 10g, Fiber: 1g

INGREDIENTS

1 cup cooked sweet potato, mashed
1 cup chopped fresh spinach
1/2 cup oat flour
1 egg

DIRECTIONS

1. Set the oven temperature at 350°F(175°C), and line a sheet of parchment paper with it.
2. Mix the mashed sweet potato, chopped spinach, oat flour, and egg in a medium bowl.
3. Spread the mixture evenly on the prepared baking sheet.
4. Bake for 25 minutes or until firm and golden brown.
5. Allow cooling completely before cutting into squares.

Pea and Carrot Balls

35 minutes

12-14 Treats

NUTRITIONAL VALUES

Calories: 30, Protein: 2g, Fat: 1g, Carbohydrates: 4g, Fiber: 1g

INGREDIENTS

1 cup frozen peas, thawed
1/2 cup grated carrots
1/2 cup oat flour
1 egg

DIRECTIONS

1. Set the oven temperature at 350°F(175°C) and line a sheet of parchment paper with it.
2. In a food processor, pulse the peas until they are finely chopped.
3. Mix the chopped peas, grated carrots, oat flour, and egg in a medium bowl.
4. Use a spoon or cookie scoop to form the mixture into small balls.
5. Set the balls on the prepared baking sheet and bake for 20 minutes or until firm and lightly browned.
6. Allow cooling completely before serving.

Sweet Potato and Cranberry Bites

40 minutes

18 Treats

NUTRITIONAL VALUES

Calories: 45, Protein: 2g, Fat: 1g, Carbohydrates: 8g, Fiber: 1g1g

INGREDIENTS

1 cup cooked sweet potato, mashed
1/2 cup dried cranberries, chopped
1/2 cup oat flour
1 egg

DIRECTIONS

1. Set the oven temperature at 350°F(175°C) and line a sheet of parchment paper with it.
2. Mix the mashed sweet potato, chopped cranberries, oat flour, and egg in a medium bowl.
3. Use a spoon or cookie scoop to form the mixture into small balls or shapes.
4. Place the bites on the prepared baking sheet and bake for 25 minutes or until firm and lightly browned.
5. Allow cooling completely before serving.

Lentil and Spinach Bars

45 minutes

16-18 Treats

NUTRITIONAL VALUES

Calories: 65, Protein: 4g, Fat: 1g, Carbohydrates: 11g, Fiber: 2g

INGREDIENTS

1 cup cooked lentils
1 cup chopped fresh spinach
1/2 cup oat flour
1 egg

DIRECTIONS

1. Turn the oven temperature to 350°F (175°C) and line a sheet of parchment paper with it.
2. In a food processor, pulse the cooked lentils until they are finely chopped.
3. Mix the chopped lentils, spinach, oat flour, and egg in a medium bowl.
4. Spread the mixture evenly on the prepared baking sheet.
5. Bake for 30 minutes or until firm and lightly browned.
6. Allow cooling completely before cutting into bars.

Chickpea and Pumpkin Cookies

35 minutes

22-24 Treats

NUTRITIONAL VALUES

Calories: 35, Protein: 2g, Fat: 1g, Carbohydrates: 6g, Fiber: 2g

INGREDIENTS

1 cup canned chickpeas, drained and rinsed
1/2 cup canned pumpkin puree
1/2 cup oat flour
1/2 tsp ground cinnamon
1 egg

DIRECTIONS

1. Turn the oven temperature to 350°F (175°C) and line a sheet of parchment paper with it.
2. Chickpeas can be finely minced in a food processor.
3. Combine chopped chickpeas, pumpkin puree, oat flour, cinnamon, and egg in a medium bowl.
4. Use a spoon or biscuit scoop to make little cookies.
5. Put the cookieson the baking sheet that has been prepared and bake them for 20 minutes or until they are firm and lightly browned.
6. Allow cooling completely before serving.

Banana Oatmeal Dog Treats

35 minutes | **20-22 Treats**

NUTRITIONAL VALUES

Calories: 60, Protein: 3g, Fat: 4g, Carbohydrates: 4g, Fiber: 1g, Sugar: 2g

INGREDIENTS

2 ripe bananas, mashed
2 cups rolled oats
1 cup whole wheat flour
1/4 cup unsweetened applesauce
1 egg

DIRECTIONS

1. Preheat the oven to 350F (175°C) and arrange the baking sheet with parchment paper.
2. Combine the mashed bananas, rolled oats, whole wheat flour, applesauce, and egg in a large bowl.
3. Mix until a dough forms, adding a little water if necessary.
4. Roll the dough out over the smooth surface to a 1/4-inch thickness and cut into desired shapes using a cookie cutter, or form small balls and flatten them slightly.
5. Place the treats on the paper-arranged baking sheet.
6. Bake for 23-25 minutes or until golden and firm.
7. Allow the banana oatmeal dog treats to cool on a wire rack before serving.

Broccoli and Apple Squares

35 minutes

12 treats

NUTRITIONAL VALUES

Calories: 55, Protein: 2g, Fat: 1g, Carbohydrates: 10g, Fiber: 2g

INGREDIENTS

1 cup cooked broccoli, finely chopped
1 cup grated apple
1/2 cup oat flour
1 egg

DIRECTIONS

1. Prepare a parchment-lined baking sheet and preheat the oven to 350°F (175°C).
2. Mix the chopped broccoli, grated apple, oat flour, and egg in a medium bowl.
3. Spread the mixture evenly on the prepared baking sheet.
4. Bake for 25 minutes or until firm and lightly browned.
5. Allow cooling completely before cutting into squares.

Spinach and Blueberry Biscuits

35 minutes

18 treats

NUTRITIONAL VALUES

Calories: 50, Protein: 2g, Fat: 1g, Carbohydrates: 9g, Fiber: 1g

INGREDIENTS

1 cup oat flour
1/2 cup chopped fresh spinach
1/2 cup fresh blueberries
1 egg

DIRECTIONS

1. Heat the oven to 350°F (175°C) and line a pan with parchment paper.
2. Pulse the spinach and oat flour in a food processor until blended.
3. Add blueberries and pulse until finely chopped.
4. In a larger bowl, whisk the egg and blueberry mixture.
5. Add the oat flour mixture to the bowl and stir until a dough forms.
6. Use a biscuit cutter to make biscuits from 1/4-inch dough.
7. Bake for 20 minutes until firm and gently browned.
8. Allow cooling completely before serving.

Special Diet Treats

Allergy-Friendly Chicken and Rice Cookies

40 minutes

24 Treats

NUTRITIONAL VALUES

Calories: 45cal, Protein: 3g, Fat: 1g, Carbohydrates: 5g, Fiber: 1g

INGREDIENTS

1 cup cooked chicken, finely chopped
1 cup cooked brown rice
1/4 cup oat flour
1 egg

DIRECTIONS

1. Set the oven temperature to 350°F (175°C) and line a baking surface with parchment paper.
2. Mix the chopped chicken, cooked rice, oat flour, and egg in a medium bowl.
3. Use a spoon or cookie scoop to form the mixture into small cookies.
4. Arrange the cookies on the baking sheet and place them in the oven for 25 minutes.
5. Allow cooling completely before serving.

Very Berry Low Fat Dog Treats

35 minutes

24 treats

NUTRITIONAL VALUES

Calories: 48, Protein: 2g, Fat: 1g, Carbohydrates: 9g, Fiber: 1g

INGREDIENTS

2 cups whole wheat flour
1/2 cup rolled oats
1 cup mixed berries (blueberries, raspberries, or chopped strawberries)
1 egg
1/2 cup low-fat plain yogurt

DIRECTIONS

1. Preheat the oven to 350F (175°C) and arrange the baking sheet with parchment paper.
2. Combine whole wheat flour, rolled oats, mixed berries, egg, and low-fat plain yogurt in a large bowl.
3. Mix until a dough forms, adding a little water if necessary.
4. Roll the dough out over the smooth surface to a 1/4-inch thickness and cut into desired shapes using a cookie cutter.
5. Place the treats on the paper-arranged baking sheet and bake for 23-25 minutes or until golden and crisp.
6. Allow the very berry, low-fat dog treats to cool before serving.

Grilled Sweet Potato

30 minutes

4-6 Treats

NUTRITIONAL VALUES

Calories: 108, Protein: 2g, Fat: 1g,
Carbohydrates: 25g, Fiber: 4g

INGREDIENTS

2 sweet potatoes, washed and sliced into 1/2-inch rounds
1 tablespoon olive oil
Pinch of salt (optional)

DIRECTIONS

1. Preheat your grill to medium heat.
2. Toss the sweet potato rounds with olive oil and salt if using.
3. Place the sweet potato rounds on the grill and cook for 5-7 minutes for each side or until tender and slightly charred.
4. Allow the grilled sweet potato to cool before serving.

Digestive-Friendly Pumpkin and Ginger Treats

40 minutes

8-10 treat

NUTRITIONAL VALUES

Calories: 20cal, Protein: 1g, Fat: 1g, Carbohydrates: 4g, Fiber: 2g

INGREDIENTS

1/2 cup canned pumpkin
1/4 cup coconut flour
1/4 cup oat flour
1 tsp grated fresh ginger

DIRECTIONS

1. Set the oven temperature to 350°F (175°C) and line a baking surface with parchment paper.
2. Mix the pumpkin, coconut flour, oat flour, and grated ginger in a medium bowl.
3. Use a spoon or cookie scoop to form the mixture into small balls or any shapes.
4. Put the treats on the prepared baking sheet and place them in the oven for 25 minutes.
5. Allow cooling completely before serving.

Turkey and Green Bean Bites

35 minutes

20 Treats

NUTRITIONAL VALUES

Calories: 45cal, Protein: 4g, Fat: 2g, Carbohydrates: 3g, Fiber: 1g

INGREDIENTS

1 cup cooked ground turkey
1 cup cooked green beans, finely chopped
1/2 cup almond flour
1 egg

DIRECTIONS

1. Set the oven temperature to 350°F (175°C) and line a baking surface with parchment paper.
2. Mix the cooked ground turkey, chopped green beans, almond flour, and egg in a medium bowl.
3. Use a spoon or cookie scoop to form the mixture into small bites.
4. Place the bites on the prepared baking sheet and bake for 20 minutes or until it gets firm and lightly browned.
5. Allow cooling completely before serving.

Low-Fat Chicken and Carrot Bars

45 minutes

12 Treats

NUTRITIONAL VALUES

Calories: 45cal, Protein: 4g, Fat: 1g, Carbohydrates: 6g, Fiber: 1g

INGREDIENTS

1 cup cooked chicken, finely shredded
1 cup grated carrots
1/2 cup oat flour
1 egg

DIRECTIONS

1. Set the oven temperature to 350°F (175°C) and prepare a baking dish with parchment.
2. Combine the shredded chicken, grated carrots, oat flour, and egg in a medium basin.
3. In the prepared baking dish, pour the ingredients.
4. Bake for 30 minutes or until firm and lightly browned.
5. Allow cooling completely before cutting into bars.

Dental Health Beef and Parsley Jerky

3 hours

14 Treats

NUTRITIONAL VALUES

Calories: 35cal, Protein: 5g, Fat: 1g, Carbohydrates: 0g, Fiber: 0g

INGREDIENTS

1 lb lean beef, sliced thinly
1/2 cup dried parsley

DIRECTIONS

1. Set the oven temperature to 350°F (175°C) and prepare a baking dish with waxed paper.
2. Lay the beef slices out on the prepared baking sheet.
3. Sprinkle the dried parsley over the beef.
4. Bake for 3 hours or until the beef is completely dried out.
5. Allow cooling completely before serving.

Low-Calorie Tuna and Cucumber Bites

10 minutes

24 Treats

NUTRITIONAL VALUES

Calories: 15cal, Protein: 2g, Fat: 0g, Carbohydrates: 1g, Fiber: 0g

INGREDIENTS

1/2 cup canned tuna, drained and flaked
1 large cucumber
1 tsp lemon juice

DIRECTIONS

1. Mix the tuna with lemon juice in a medium bowl.
2. Wash and clean the cucumber, cut cucumber into 1/2 inch thick round pieces.
3. Top each cucumber piece with tuna mixture. Chill pieces for 1-2 hours (if needed) then serve to you dog.

Joint Health Lamb and Turmeric Cookies

35 minutes

20-22 Treats

NUTRITIONAL VALUES

Calories: 50cal, Protein: 4g, Fat: 2g, Carbohydrates: 3g, Fiber: 1g

INGREDIENTS

1 cup cooked ground lamb
1/2 cup grated carrots
1/2 cup oat flour
1 tsp ground turmeric

DIRECTIONS

1. Set the oven temperature to 350°F (175°C) and line a baking surface with parchment paper.
2. Mix the cooked ground lamb, grated carrots, oat flour, and ground turmeric in a medium bowl.
3. Use a spoon or cookie scoop to form the mixture into small cookies.
4. Put your cookies on the prepared baking sheet and bake for 20 minutes or until they get lightly browned.
5. Allow cooling completely before serving.

Skin and Coat Chicken and Coconut Bars

40 minutes

12 Treats

NUTRITIONAL VALUES

Calories: 45cal, Protein: 4g, Fat: 2g, Carbohydrates: 5g, Fiber: 1g

INGREDIENTS

1 cup cooked chicken, finely chopped
1/2 cup shredded coconut
1/2 cup oat flour
1 egg

DIRECTIONS

1. Set the oven temperature to 350°F (175°C) and prepare a baking dish with waxed paper.
2. Mix the chopped chicken, shredded coconut, oat flour, and egg in a medium bowl.
3. Spread the blending evenly in the prepared baking dish.
4. Bake for 25 minutes or until firm and lightly browned.
5. Allow cooling completely before cutting into bars.

Grain-Sensitive Sweet Potato and Quinoa Biscuits

45 minutes

16-18 Treats

NUTRITIONAL VALUES

Calories: 35cal, Protein: 2g, Fat: 1g, Carbohydrates: 5g, Fiber: 1g

INGREDIENTS

1 cup cooked sweet potato, mashed
1/2 cup cooked quinoa
1/4 cup oat flour
1 egg

DIRECTIONS

1. Set the oven temperature to 350°F (175°C) and line a baking surface with parchment paper.
2. Mix the mashed sweet potato, cooked quinoa, oat flour, and egg in a medium bowl.
3. Use a spoon or cookie scoop to form the mixture into small biscuits.
4. Put the biscuits on the prepared baking sheet and bake for 30 minutes or until lightly browned.
5. Allow cooling completely before serving.

Diabetic-Friendly Chicken and Apple Treats

45 minutes **16-18 Treats**

NUTRITIONAL VALUES

Calories: 35cal, Protein: 3g, Fat: 2g, Carbohydrates: 2g, Fiber: 1g

INGREDIENTS

1 cup cooked chicken, ground
1/2 cup grated apple
1/4 cup almond flour
1 egg

DIRECTIONS

1. Set the oven temperature to 350°F (175°C) and line a baking surface with parchment paper.
2. Mix the ground chicken, grated apple, almond flour, and egg in a medium bowl.
3. Use a spoon or cookie scoop to form the mixture into small treats.
4. Put the treats on the prepared baking sheet and bake for 20 minutes or until lightly gets browned.
5. Allow cooling completely before serving.

Gluten-Free Beef and Potato Squares

40 minutes

20 Treats

NUTRITIONAL VALUES

Calories: 45cal, Protein: 4g, Fat: 2g, Carbohydrates: 5g, Fiber: 1g

INGREDIENTS

1 cup cooked ground beef
1 cup mashed potato
1/4 cup oat flour
1 egg

DIRECTIONS

1. Set the oven temperature to 350°F (175°C) and line a baking surface with parchment paper.
2. Mix the cooked ground beef, mashed potato, oat flour, and egg in a medium bowl.
3. Spread the mixture evenly on the prepared baking sheet.
4. Bake for 25 minutes or until firm and lightly browned.
5. Allow cooling completely before cutting into squares.

Vegetarian Lentil and Carrot Balls

40 minutes

16-18 Treats

NUTRITIONAL VALUES

Calories: 30cal, Protein: 2g, Fat: 1g, Carbohydrates: 4g, Fiber: 1g

INGREDIENTS

1 cup cooked lentils, drained and mashed
1/2 cup grated carrot
1/4 cup oat flour
1 egg

DIRECTIONS

1. Set the oven temperature to 350°F (175°C) and line a baking surface with parchment paper.
2. Mix the mashed lentils, grated carrot, oat flour, and egg in a medium bowl.
3. Use a spoon or cookie scoop to form the mixture into small balls.
4. Put the cookies on the greased baking sheet and place them in the oven for 25 minutes.
5. Allow cooling completely before serving

Picky Eater Chicken and Cheese Bars

40 minutes

12 Treats

NUTRITIONAL VALUES

Calories: 50cal, Protein: 4g, Fat: 3g, Carbohydrates: 2g, Fiber: 0g

INGREDIENTS

1 cup cooked chicken, finely chopped
1/2 cup shredded cheddar cheese
1/4 cup oat flour
1 egg

DIRECTIONS

1. Set the oven temperature to 350°F (175°C) and line a baking surface with parchment paper.
2. Mix the chopped chicken, shredded cheddar cheese, oat flour, and egg in a medium bowl.
3. Spread the mixture evenly on the prepared baking sheet.
4. Bake for 25 minutes or until firm and lightly browned.
5. Allow cooling completely before cutting into bars.

Snacks Treats

Peanut Butter and Banana Biscuits

30 minutes

8-10 Treats

NUTRITIONAL VALUES

Calories: 50cal, Protein: 2g, Fat: 3g, Carbohydrates: 4g, Fiber: 1g

INGREDIENTS

1 ripe banana, mashed
1/4 cup natural peanut butter
1/2 cup oat flour

DIRECTIONS

1. Set the oven temperature to 350°F (175°C) and line a sheet of parchment paper with it.
2. Mix the mashed banana, natural peanut butter, and oat flour in a medium bowl.
3. Use a spoon or cookie scoop to form the mixture into small biscuits.
4. Put the balls on the sheet of parchment paper and bake for 20 minutes until lightly browned.
5. Allow cooling completely before s Chicken and Sweet Potato Balls erving.

Cheesy Bacon Bites

30 minutes

14 Treats

NUTRITIONAL VALUES

Calories: 35cal, Protein: 3g, Fat: 2g, Carbohydrates: 1g, Fiber: 0g

INGREDIENTS

1/2 cup cooked and crumbled bacon
1/2 cup shredded cheddar cheese
1/4 cup oat flour

DIRECTIONS

1. Set the oven temperature to 350°F (175°C) and line a sheet of parchment paper with it.
2. Mix the cooked and crumbled bacon, shredded cheddar cheese, and oat flour in a medium bowl.
3. Use a spoon or cookie scoop to form the mixture into small bites.
4. Put the balls on the sheet of parchment paper and bake for 20 minutes until lightly browned.
5. Allow cooling completely before serving.

Chicken and Rice Balls

35 minutes

16-18 Treats

NUTRITIONAL VALUES

Calories: 30cal, Protein: 3g, Fat: 1g, Carbohydrates: 2g, Fiber: 0g

INGREDIENTS

1 cup cooked chicken, shredded
1/2 cup cooked brown rice
1/4 cup oat flour
1 egg

DIRECTIONS

1. Set the oven temperature to 350°F (175°C) and line a sheet of parchment paper with it.
2. Mix the shredded cooked chicken, brown rice, oat flour, and egg in a medium bowl.
3. Use a spoon or cookie scoop to form the mixture into small balls.
4. Put the balls on the sheet of parchment paper and bake for 20 minutes until lightly browned.
5. Allow cooling completely before serving.

Carrot and Apple Cookies

35 minutes | **14 Treats**

NUTRITIONAL VALUES

Calories: 25cal, Protein: 1g, Fat: 1g, Carbohydrates: 3g, Fiber: 0g

INGREDIENTS

1/2 cup grated carrot
1/2 cup grated apple
1/4 cup oat flour
1 egg

DIRECTIONS

1. Set the oven temperature to 350°F (175°C) and line a sheet of parchment paper with it.
2. Mix the grated carrot, apple, oat flour, and egg in a medium bowl.
3. Use a spoon or cookie scoop to form the mixture into small cookies.
4. Put the balls on the sheet of parchment paper and bake for 20 minutes until lightly browned.
5. Allow cooling completely before serving.

Sweet Potato and Cinnamon Treats

35 minutes

12 Treats

NUTRITIONAL VALUES

Calories: 20cal, Protein: 1g, Fat: 0g, Carbohydrates: 4g, Fiber: 1g

INGREDIENTS

1 cup cooked and mashed sweet potato
1/4 cup oat flour
1/2 teaspoon ground cinnamon

DIRECTIONS

1. Set the oven temperature to 350°F (175°C) and line a sheet of parchment paper with it.
2. Mix the mashed sweet potato, oat flour, and ground cinnamon in a medium bowl.
3. Use a spoon or cookie scoop to form the mixture into small treats.
4. Put the balls on the sheet of parchment paper and bake for 20 minutes until lightly browned.
5. Allow cooling completely before serving

Blueberry and Yogurt Squares

40 minutes

14-16 Treats

NUTRITIONAL VALUES

Calories: 20cal, Protein: 1g, Fat: 1g, Carbohydrates: 2g, Fiber: 0g

INGREDIENTS

1/2 cup fresh blueberries
1/2 cup plain Greek yogurt
1/4 cup oat flour
1 egg

DIRECTIONS

1. Set the oven temperature to 350°F (175°C) and line a sheet of parchment paper with it.
2. Mix the fresh blueberries, plain Greek yogurt, oat flour, and egg in a medium bowl.
3. Pour the blending into a baking dish and bake for 30 minutes or until set.
4. Allow cooling completely before slicing into small squares.

Beef and Cheddar Bars

35 minutes

14 Treats

NUTRITIONAL VALUES

Calories: 40cal, Protein: 5g, Fat: 2g, Carbohydrates: 1g, Fiber: 0g

INGREDIENTS

1/2 cup cooked and chopped lean beef
1/2 cup shredded cheddar cheese
1/4 cup oat flour
1 egg

DIRECTIONS

1. Set the oven temperature to 350°F (175°C) and line a sheet of parchment paper with it.
2. Mix the cooked and chopped lean beef, shredded cheddar cheese, oat flour, and egg in a medium bowl.
3. Use a spoon or cookie scoop to form the mixture into small bars.
4. Put the balls on the sheet of parchment paper and bake for 20 minutes until lightly browned.
5. Allow cooling completely before serving.

Fried Fish Skin

15 minutes **4-6 Treats**

NUTRITIONAL VALUES

Calories: 117, Protein: 11g, Fat: 8g, Carbohydrates: 0g, Fiber: 0g

INGREDIENTS

Fish skin from 2-3 large fish, such as salmon or cod
1 tablespoon olive oil

DIRECTIONS

1. Heat one tbsp oil in a large skillet over medium heat.
2. Add the fish skin, skin-side down, and cook for 4-6 minutes or until crispy and golden.
3. Flip and cook for an additional 2-3 minutes.
4. Allow the fried fish skin to cool before serving.

Air Fried Pork Rinds

20 minutes

4-6 Treats

NUTRITIONAL VALUES

Calories: 119, Protein: 11g, Fat: 8g, Carbohydrates: 0g, Fiber: 0g

INGREDIENTS

1 lb. pork skin, cut into 1-inch squares

DIRECTIONS

1. Preheat your air fryer to 400°F (200°C).
2. Place the pork skin squares in a single layer in the air fryer basket.
3. Cook for 15-20 minutes or until the pork rinds are crispy and golden.
4. Allow the air-fried pork rinds to cool before serving.

Salmon and Dill Biscuits

40 minutes

8-10 Treats

NUTRITIONAL VALUES

Calories: 35cal, Protein: 3g, Fat: 1g, Carbohydrates: 3g, Fiber: 0g

INGREDIENTS

1/2 cup cooked and mashed salmon
1/2 cup oat flour
1 tablespoon chopped fresh dill

DIRECTIONS

1. Set the oven temperature to 350°F (175°C) and line a sheet of parchment paper
2. with it. Mix the cooked and mashed salmon, oat flour, and chopped fresh dill in a medium bowl.
3. Use a spoon or cookie scoop to form the mixture into small biscuits.
4. Put the balls on the sheet of parchment paper and bake for 20 minutes until lightly browned.
5. Allow cooling completely before serving.

Dried Beef Stomach

8-10 hours

10-12 pieces

NUTRITIONAL VALUES

Calories: 95, Protein: 15g, Fat: 9g, Carbohydrates: 0g, Fiber: 0g

INGREDIENTS

2 lb. beef tripe

DIRECTIONS

1. Preheat your oven to 170°F (77°C) or the lowest possible setting.
2. Clean and trim the tripe, removing any excess fat.
3. Slice the tripe into ¼-inch thick strips.
4. Arrange the strips on a wire rack placed on a baking sheet.
5. Bake for 8-10 hours or until the tripe is fully dried and crispy.
6. Allow the dried beef stomach to cool before serving.

Air Fried Bacon Strips

10 minutes **6-8 strips**

NUTRITIONAL VALUES

Calories: 350, Protein: 25g, Fat: 9g, Carbohydrates: 45g, Fiber: 6g

INGREDIENTS

6-8 bacon strips (preferably low sodium)

DIRECTIONS

1. Preheat your air fryer to 400°F (200°C).
2. Lay the bacon strips in one layer in the air fryer basket, avoiding overlap.
3. Cook for 8-10 minutes or until the bacon is crispy.
4. Allow the bacon strips to cool before serving.

Carrot and Cheese Treats

35 minutes

16-18 Treats

NUTRITIONAL VALUES

Calories: 35cal, Protein: 3g, Fat: 2g, Carbohydrates: 2g, Fiber: 0g

INGREDIENTS

1 cup grated carrot
1/2 cup shredded cheddar cheese
1/4 cup oat flour
1 egg

DIRECTIONS

1. Set the oven temperature to 350°F (175°C) and line a sheet of parchment paper with it.
2. Mix the grated carrot, shredded cheddar cheese, oat flour, and egg in a medium bowl.
3. Use a spoon or cookie scoop to form the mixture into small treats.
4. Put the balls on the sheet of parchment paper and bake for 20 minutes until lightly browned.
5. Allow cooling completely before serving.

Dry Dog Snack

50 minutes

20-24 Treats

NUTRITIONAL VALUES

Calories: 350, Protein: 25g, Fat: 9g, Carbohydrates: 45g, Fiber: 6g

INGREDIENTS

4 cups whole wheat flour
1 cup powdered milk
1 cup cooked brown rice
1 cup cooked and mashed sweet potato
2 cups boiled ground chicken
1/4 cup olive oil

DIRECTIONS

1. Mix the whole wheat flour, powdered milk, brown rice, sweet potato, ground meat, and olive oil in a large bowl.
2. Form the mixture evenly into small balls and allow the dry dog food to rest before serving to your pet.

Peanut Butter Carob Cups

30 minutes

12 cups

NUTRITIONAL VALUES

Calories: 149, Protein: 3g, Fat: 12g, Carbohydrates: 9g, Fiber: 2g

INGREDIENTS

1 cup carob chips
1/2 cup unsweetened peanut butter
12 silicone or paper cupcake liners

DIRECTIONS

1. Melt the carob chips in a microwave-safe bowl or a double boiler until smooth.
2. Place a spoonful of melted carob in each cupcake liner, spreading it to cover the bottom.
3. Spoon the peanut butter on top of the carob layer in each cup.
4. Pour another layer of melted carob over the peanut butter, fully covering it.
5. Place the cups in the refrigerator for at least 20 minutes or until the carob has set.
6. Remove the carob cups from the liners before serving.

Grain Free Treats

Bully Sticks

1 hour

6-8 sticks

NUTRITIONAL VALUES

Calories: 170, Protein: 44g, Fat: 0g, Carbohydrates: 0g, Fiber: 0g

INGREDIENTS

6-8 beef pizzles (bull penis)

DIRECTIONS

1. Preheat the oven to 250°F (120°C)).
2. Rinse the pizzle thoroughly and pat dry with paper towels.
3. Cut the pizzle into 6-8 inch sticks.
4. Place the sticks on a baking sheet lined with parchment paper.
5. Bake for 53-60 minutes or until the sticks are fully dried and hardened.
6. Allow the bully sticks to cool before serving.

Sweet Potato and Turkey Jerky

4 hours

12-14 Treats

NUTRITIONAL VALUES

Calories: 35, Protein: 4g, Fat: 1g, Carbohydrates: 4g, Fiber: 1g

INGREDIENTS

2 sweet potatoes, sliced thinly
1/2 pound cooked turkey breast, sliced thinly

DIRECTIONS

1. Prepare a parchment-lined baking sheet and preheat the oven to 200°F (93°C).
2. Arrange the sweet potato and turkey slices on the prepared baking sheet, alternating between the two.
3. Bake for 4 hours or until the jerky is dry and crispy.
4. Allow cooling completely before serving.

Chickpea and Carrot Balls

35 minutes

18-20 Treats

NUTRITIONAL VALUES

Calories: 40, Protein: 3g, Fat: 2g, Carbohydrates: 4g, Fiber: 1g

INGREDIENTS

1 cup canned chickpeas, drained and rinsed
1/2 cup grated carrots
1/2 cup almond flour
1 egg

DIRECTIONS

1. Prepare a parchment-lined baking sheet and preheat the oven to 350°F (175°C).
2. Pulse chickpeas in a blender until finely minced.
3. Combine chopped chickpeas, grated carrots, almond flour, and egg in a medium bowl.
4. Make balls with a spoon or biscuit scoop.
5. Bake for 20 minutes until firm and gently browned.
6. Allow cooling completely before serving.

Dried Beef Lungs

6-8 hours

10 pieces

NUTRITIONAL VALUES

Calories: 97, Protein: 17g, Fat: 3g, Carbohydrates: 0g, Fiber: 0g

INGREDIENTS

2 lb. beef lungs

DIRECTIONS

1. Preheat your oven to 170°F (77°C) or the lowest possible setting.
2. Rinse the beef lungs and pat them dry with paper towels.
3. Cut the lungs into ¼-inch thick slices.
4. Arrange the slices on a wire rack placed on a baking sheet.
5. Bake for 6-8 hours or until the lung slices are fully dried and crisp.
6. Allow the dried beef lungs to cool before serving.

Dog Cupcakes

30 minutes

12 cupcakes

NUTRITIONAL VALUES

Calories: 102, Protein: 2g, Fat: 3g, Carbohydrates: 16g, Fiber: 1g

INGREDIENTS

1 egg
¼ cup unsweetened applesauce
¼ cup honey
½ cup whole wheat flour
1 teaspoon baking powder

DIRECTIONS

1. Preheat the oven to 350°F (175°C) and arrange the 12-cup muffin tin with paper liners.
2. Whisk together the egg, applesauce, and honey in a large bowl.
3. Add the whole wheat flour and baking powder, mixing until combined.
4. Spoon the batter into the arranged cups, filling each about 2/3 full.
5. Bake for 17-20 minutes or until a tooth stick inserted into the center comes clean.
6. Allow the cupcakes to cool before serving.

Fried Beef Liver

20 minutes

4-6 Treats

NUTRITIONAL VALUES

Calories: 150, Protein: 24g, Fat: 5g, Carbohydrates: 2g, Fiber: 0g

INGREDIENTS

1 lb. beef liver, sliced
1 tablespoon olive oil

DIRECTIONS

1. Heat one tbsp oil in a large skillet over medium heat.
2. Add the beef liver slices and cook for 5-7 minutes for each side until browned and cooked.
3. Allow the fried liver to cool before serving.

Chickpea and Blueberry Squares

40 minutes

16-18 Treats

NUTRITIONAL VALUES

Calories: 45, Protein: 2g, Fat: 2g, Carbohydrates: 5g, Fiber: 2g

INGREDIENTS

1 cup canned chickpeas, drained and rinsed
1/2 cup fresh blueberries
1/2 cup almond flour
1 egg

DIRECTIONS

1. Prepare a parchment-lined baking dish and preheat the oven to 350°F (175°C).
2. Pulse chickpeas in a blender until finely minced.
3. Combine chopped chickpeas, blueberries, almond flour, and egg in a medium bowl.
4. Distribute the mixture in the baking dish.
5. Bake for 25 minutes or until firm and lightly browned.
6. Allow cooling completely before cutting into squares.

Lentil and Broccoli Cookies

35 minutes

24-26 Treats

NUTRITIONAL VALUES

Calories: 45, Protein: 3g, Fat: 1g, Carbohydrates: 6g, Fiber: 3g

INGREDIENTS

1 cup cooked lentils
1 cup cooked broccoli, finely chopped
1/2 cup coconut flour
1 egg

DIRECTIONS

1. Prepare a wax paper baking sheet and preheat the oven to 350°F (175°C).
2. Pulse cooked lentils in a food processor until finely minced.
3. Combine chopped lentils, broccoli, coconut flour, and egg in a medium bowl.
4. Make cookies with a spoon or biscuit scoop.
5. Bake the cookies for 20 minutes until firm and gently browned.
6. Allow cooling completely before serving.

Peanut Butter and Pumpkin Bones

45 minutes

24 Treats

NUTRITIONAL VALUES

Calories: 113, Protein: 4g, Fat: 4g, Carbohydrates: 16g, Fiber: 2g

INGREDIENTS

2½ cups whole wheat flour
½ cup canned pumpkin (not pie filling)
¼ cup unsweetened peanut butter
2 eggs
¼ cup water

DIRECTIONS

1. Set the oven to 350°F (175°C) and arrange the baking sheet with parchment paper.
2. Mix the whole wheat flour, pumpkin, peanut butter, and eggs in a large bowl.
3. Gradually add water, mixing until a dough forms.
4. Roll out the dough to 1/4-inch thickness and cut out treats using a bone-shaped cookie cutter.
5. Put the treats on the paper-arranged baking sheet and bake for 25-30 minutes or until crisp and golden.
6. Allow the treats to cool before serving.

Chickpea and Beef Brownies

40 minutes

18-20 Treats

NUTRITIONAL VALUES

Calories: 55, Protein: 4g, Fat: 1g, Carbohydrates: 8g, Fiber: 2g

INGREDIENTS

1 cup canned chickpeas, drained and rinsed
1/2 cup cooked beef, finely chopped
1/2 cup oat flour
1 egg

DIRECTIONS

1. Set the oven to 350° F (175°C) and line a baking dish with parchment.
2. Use a food processor to chop the chickpeas into small pieces.
3. Combine minced meat, chickpeas, oat flour, and egg in a medium bowl.
4. Distribute the mixture in the baking dish.
5. Bake for 25 minutes or until firm and lightly browned.
6. Allow cooling completely before cutting into brownies.

Measurement Conversion Chart

Dry Measurements	
Measurement	**Equivalent**
1 Lb	16 ounces
1 cup	16 Tbsp
3/4 cup	12 Tbsp
2/3 cup	10 Tbsp plus 2 tsp
1/2 cup	8 Tbsp
3/8 cup	6 Tbsp
1/3 cup	5 Tbsp plus 1 tsp
1/4 cup	4 Tbsp
1/6 cup	2 Tbsp plus 2 tsp
1/8 cup	2 Tbsp
1/16 cup	1 Tbsp
1 Tbsp	3 tsp
1/8 tsp	Pinch
1/16 tsp	Dash
1/2 cup butter	1 stick of butter

Liquid Measurements	
Measurement	**Equivalent**
4 quarts	1 gallon
2 quarts	1/2 gallon
1 quart	1/4 gallon
2 pints	1 quart
4 cups	1 quart
2 cups	1/2 quart
2 cups	1 pint
1 cup	1/2 pint
1 cup	1/4 quart
1 cup	8 fluid ounces
3/4 cup	6 fluid ounces
2/3 cup	5.3 fluid ounces
1/2 cup	4 fluid ounces
1/3 cup	2.7 fluid ounces
1/4 cup	2 fluid ounces
1 Tbsp	0.5 fluid ounces

U.S. to Metric Conversions	
Measurement	**Metric Conversion**
Weight Measurements	
1 Lb	454 grams
8 ounces	227 grams
4 ounces	113 grams
1 ounce	28 grams
Volume Measurements	
4 quarts	3.8 liters
4 cups (1 quart)	0.95 liters
2 cups	473 milliliters
1 cup	237 milliliters
3/4 cup	177 milliliters
2/3 cup	158 milliliters
1/2 cup	118 milliliters
1/3 cup	79 milliliters
1/4 cup	59 milliliters
1/5 cup	47 milliliters
1 Tbsp	15 milliliters
1 tsp	5 milliliters
1/2 tsp	2.5 milliliters
1/5 tsp	1 milliliter
Fluid Measurements	
34 fluid ounces	1 liter
8 fluid ounces	237 milliliters
3.4 fluid ounces	100 milliliters
1 fluid ounce	30 milliliters

Oven Temperatures	
250°F	120°C
320°F	160°C
350°F	180°C
400°F	205°C
425°F	220°C

DJTS Publishing
info@djts-publishing.com

ISBN Ebook: 978-3-910634-16-9
ISBN Paperback: 978-3-910634-17-6

Imprint: DJTS Publishing

Printed in Great Britain
by Amazon

47780171R00057